If your life or perceptions of life are simplified after reading this book I would love to know your story at sujitlalwani.com.

This is a book which promises to resolve the most binding issues of the age group 14-28, though it has gained quality reception even in the higher age groups.

Thank you.

LIFE SIMPLIFIED!
Simplifying Lives Globally...

"I think this book could be extremely useful for many people making their way in life and I congratulate Sujit on having written it."

~Carole Stone, Chairman, YouGovStone
(The "Networking Queen of the World")

SUJIT LALWANI

PARTRIDGE
A Penguin Random House Company

THANK YOU GOD!

To order additional copies of this book, contact
Partridge India
000 800 10062 62
www.partridgepublishing.com/india
orders.india@partridgepublishing.com

Each quote is an original work of the author and hence any references made to these quotes would require his mention or reference. These quotes are copyright quotes of the author.

SLS
Sujit Lalwani ⇔ Life Simplified
Simplified Life ⇔ Lalwani's Suggestion

CAUTION!

Read this book as though we are talking to each other and am sharing some awesome and simple lessons with you. I will help you with a few sheets in between, where I will help you with space to share your feelings and thoughts after you finish reading every chapter.

Strictly use a pencil to note down your thoughts—as you may not be able to erase if you used a pen.

I truly believe, that Life changes with time and doesn't give us opportunities to erase our past, but this book surely will give you a chance to erase what you think today and record what you might have elevated to after a couple of years. This book is for long-term and not the near short-term time of your life.

I am sure, once we are done talking, there is lot that you will be doing. You will be living life with more elevated perceptions and have a simple solutions approach to all that you do. Hence, to record that growth, your genuineness to take note in these pages will be of utmost importance.

Thank you!

Preface

This book is a result of having travelled a lot of places, read a lot of books and met a lot of people. This whole experience of having done all of this brought me to write LIFE simplified.

The world at present stands around a chaotic corner and the only way to bring order down this chaotic street is to have men with direction who could make sense to the most arbitrary generation to come in the near future. The more complicated the life is being made, the less sense the coming generation is able to derive out of it. Owing to this I felt that there is a real need to simplify things and this book resulted.

Being bogged down with a huge shelf of books, a large amount of data & decision making in my life, I could easily conclude that for majority it's hard to read this much, travel this much and meet these many people. But if I could do it, then anyone can. If these are the reasons for my little success today, then this could mean a fortune to anyone& everyone, if I could share my secrets. This urge in me to make a difference to the youth of today, being one myself, brought me to write this book.

The issues are deeper. The things that I did in my life are inevitably needed to achieve success & we find a lot of them spending a lot of time coaching how to do these effectively. But I have always found that the underlying factor for the majority of successful people was the thirst they once developed in their life to achieve and then each one found their sources of water uniquely, including the quantity of water they derived was proportional to their thirst levels. Hence, It's wrong to learn by comparing. It's instead right to discover one-self than spend all the time understanding the world and trying to relate to it & becoming their type.

When I analysed that majority of my friends, including myself, have been often doing the same thing with a lot of books—buy them, scan them, read a few pages and store them! Yet, some books have made a massive impact on us. After deep thought on this, I decided to keep my book short enough that it is worth reading; worth an attempt to read the whole of it and long enough that it covers the major aspects.

The quotes in the book are the punches—that I believe will make dents on your mind at times, while at times fill the gaps that may exist on your mind. They are the ones you will carry as weapons during your decision making times(as most men keep referring to adages, anecdotes, quotes, references etc. during their conversations). The quotes in this book are all the part of my next upcoming book full of more powerful and profound quotes, which are elaborated with explanations.

I truly believe in ensuring you do not spend too much time reading this book; for, once you are inspired, you should be on your toes making things &growth happen for yourself. I believe this book will serve as a weapon during different times of your life. Each time you read this book after a certain set of experiences you will gather something else from the same lines. That was my greatest challenge while I was writing this, to layer it for different levels of experience, with the same set of words.

Even on a quick glance into this book you will be able to take some really positive and powerful words written on the beautiful royal letters for the emperor(that is you!). The goal of this book is to keep you up and going at all times, orienting you towards your goals, empowering your life, empowering your decisions, resolving your mental conflicts, building a solid decision making foundation on your mind, giving you an extra edge with right attitudes and eventually SIMPLIFYING YOUR LIFE.

Contents

Dedicated To My Family!

Acknowledgement

I thank the almighty for blessing me with the ability to put down my thoughts and ideas into words. I thank my family for being the strongest support by all means to make me reach this far in life. I thank all my teachers and mentors who taught me phenomenal lessons 'of' life &'in' life. I thank my wonderful wife who is a great strength and support. I thank my entire team who have by all means stuck to me through all phases of life.

I owe deep gratitude to my Grandpa, the example of unconditional love in my life, my grandma—for loving me & pampering me till date, my father—my role model, my mother—the epitome of commitment, brother & bhabi (sister in law) who have been pillaring support all my life and to my lovely wife who has been the foundation for the depth of love I understand in my life.

I also owe gratitude to myself for loving myself beyond imagination. I shall continue to do so, no matter how miserable life gets, as it generally does. LIFE still rocks!

*Road ahead
is unclear & uncertain,
But
My Vision is clear &
Intentions are certain!!!*

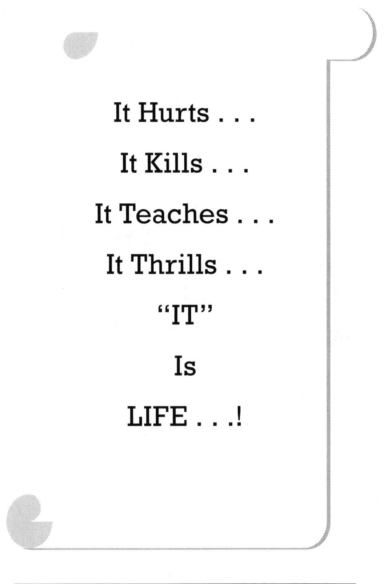

It Hurts . . .

It Kills . . .

It Teaches . . .

It Thrills . . .

"IT"

Is

LIFE . . .!

1: Hello Readers!

Around the world on all my travels, be it Zurich, Moscow, Kathmandu, Liverpool, London, Pittsburgh or many other places in India (about 300 fabulous cities/towns/villages), people have always taken liberty to build palaces of these questions on my mind—What is Life? What is the purpose of life? What is Success? What is growth? How do we set goals? How do we keep ourselves motivated? How do we stay happy in life? what should be the vision of life? Which career is the best & so on.

I do agree that I am yet to live a lot of years of my life, before I could opine on all of these. I am probably yet to experience a lot of spheres of life to give comprehensive answers to all of these, but still the journey so far has been so vast & enriching with the vast diversity of experiences on all fronts of life (spiritual, relational, professional, emotional & any other), that I find myself capable of sharing a worthy message through this unique book to impact your life. In this book, I intend to share lessons that you could imbibe for the rest of your

Every ZERO

Is

3/4th

Of an HERO . . . !

It's

All in the

PERCEPTION!

life & make happen those things you always desired. I intend to simplify life, in the ways that have been most beneficial to me.

I am positive that once you are through with this book, you can proudly look back at a great life from here on, no matter what challenges life shall pose to you in the near future.

While addressing over a million people from all walks of life, the following is a collection of perceptions I developed, which only enhanced each time I travelled more, met more people & read more books. I would be really grateful to the time you invest on reading this little book, if you would go back and find solutions to the questions that have long bothered you and no books or professors could give you solutions for the same.

Lot of us seek answers to these questions from people around us, and they bog us down with answers that have very less practical value, though their answers sound good—Like e.g., if you are bothered by a question "what do I do when I break up?"—The immediate advice from people is "Forget him/her and move on"—Definitely a great reply but not comforting or strength giving for sure, though the gist of what needs to be

The challenge of life is regretless decision making, relentless pursuit of vision with faith, forgiving others, enduring pain with a smile & achieving goals with an extra MILE.

done is in these few words; or a question like "I have lost massive money in business and am under heavy debts, what do I do?" and prompt comes the reply "It happens, get up and walk again." Definitely true, but ironically walking doesn't pay! I just mean to say one needs to have been through it or at least have had some learning on it, to be able to let you know what needs to be done, or at least help you with an advice that can make you take some concrete action that can lead you to your first few steps out of the situation.

In this book I have made my best effort to relate to what most go through and practically be of help and not make this book another "SELF HELP" Book, where after reading the entire book you feel—"awesome book! But why am I not like my cousin Ronnie, why can't I just follow my heart, am I a coward or is it that I am less talented than him . . . So on!" I want you to come out of your shell and be able to take some immediate action on your life, for, I truly believe with no action taken in life, you stand at the same place where you are, rather move behind!

This book is my little effort to ensure that, the greatest depths of life are touched in the simplest language and terminologies giving you & the readers around the globe

Love begets glory,

Work begets story.

LOVED WORK

Begets

A Story of Glory!

the scope for taking best lessons in one sitting. These will be perceptions you could fearlessly carry &I am sure they shall remain unchallenged, to empower you, keep you up with loads of confidence, throughout your life!

You have just one life & trust me you don't need many to know "Life is truly mean!" ☺ So the only way out is to make sure you make Life 'meaningful! ☺

Felt honoured to be awarded one of the youngest man around the state for high service to society & quality leadership, by LIONS Club. Each one of you can do a lot more than what you are already doing, once you are inspired!

At the Lions Club District Level Meet

At the Global Entrepreneurship Congress 2012 in UK.

Photo Credits: Melissa Stewart

With Sir Richard Branson(Founder, Virgin Group)

Stop walking with
a 'calendar'.
It's capable of ruining
your fate,
by showing you
the date
& limiting your
courage,
by reminding
you of your age.

2: LIFE & its Purpose!

Before I begin sharing my views on this vast oceanic topic, I would just love to share something really trivial but amazing: If after reading the title of the book you are expecting that 'Life gets easy' is what I am going to coach you through this book (whether after reading this book or ever due to any other reason) then you have possibly lost your money. Let me not cheat you, unlike all others you met thus far who told you life will someday get better, keep faith, keep hope, it will get easier etc. I am truly sorry, I mean it when I say "LIFE NEVER GETs EASY!"; Indeed, It was never meant to.

Life is meant to get interesting, it's meant to be made interesting, it's meant to be celebrated for all its high & low tides, it's supposed to be enjoyed whether you are taken through the Green landscapes or arid deserts, it's meant to be LOVED and that is the only goal of life.

Most people who meet me after my sessions/talks bring to my notice a never ending list of problems in their life that they feel are possibly the toughest ones relative to

Result of

HARDWORK

Is

Neither friends

Nor enemy,

To the

'AGE'

Of the

ACHIEVER!

any of their peers' problems. All others in their life seem to have a justification for what they are going through, except them. All of us feel this at some point of our life or rather pretty often, when we are going through problems; We justify with high rationality, why we are the only one going through it without any logic and all the others going through the same/similar problem have a definite logic or at least have one factor that makes it easy for them to go through it unlike our life.

Hence it brings us to a question, why do we go through what we do? What are problems? What is life itself?

Here I would love to quote my favourite line on life I once shared at one of my workshops, that *"Life indeed is a tricky game, a maze unsolvable, a game with no clear objectives and a journey with totally undefined destination."* "Different people, different perceptions" is the adage most popular about life; A saint might tell you salvation is the objective of life, while a religious guru of another form might move you towards enlightenment & fulfilment, a scientist might push you towards research, an educationist towards education, musician towards music& so on.

The wisdom of
LIFE eludes
even the best . . .

For those
who pass the test
Life is a fest,

While, it's forever,
A battle for the rest . . .

In my simplest observation & description of what I have by far learnt in my life, from my experiences,& in most cases found it deeply applicable, is this simple and highly elucidating definition of life that

"Life is a symbolic representation of a story, that is elongated in time frame, filled with diverse emotions, ethics& values, a movie by & large with defined beginning &a completely uncertain end with the sole objectives being happiness & GROWTH."

Growth of happiness & Growth of any sphere that you put your foot into or any field you put your hands into, are the sole objectives of life.

The greatest truth of life is 'Everything grows'—The universe is expanding, the trees grow from a seed to a huge structure with leaves, stem, branches and fruits, time ticks forward, nails grow no matter how many times you cut them, hair grows, companies grow, acceleration increases speed, Age increases, Cells multiply etc. Each thing relative to its previous existence seems to grow in measure.

Hence, in my simplest observation GROWTH is the foundation for life, and achieving growth in everything

The two

toughest lessons

to learn

In life

are

"LET GO"

&

"LET's GO..!"

we step into or get involved in (or get pushed into owing to situations & circumstances) must be the purpose of life. It is arguable that *everything grows to die* so why grow at all? Reminds of the legendary composition: "In the end, it doesn't even matter . . ."; Indeed, that is the truth & by observing nature around us, it's quite a fact that all that is born perishes at some point, but this in no way still defies the truth that growth is the purpose of 'life', and we need to work towards it till we are alive& till we meet death in the face.

If you are a student growth in your education is something you should/would strive for, as a teacher you would/should strive to be the best till you retire, as a businessman you should/would strive to develop your company, business, products, services and your vision, as a guru/saint/speaker you would/should increase your followers, your positive impact on the world, harmony, peace & be a reason for bringing more happiness amongst people, as a homemaker you need to grow in your care, love and concern for the family, be a reason for better health and bonding of family, as a bureaucrat you need to think of progress of your country and countrymen& so on.

When

you are stressed

on mind...

to pour it out,

is the behaviour,

most kind!

To me personally this is the simplest definition of life. This is an excerpt from my upcoming books. For greater depth, you can grab your copy once it's in the market. But here, this depth is sufficient. It's crystal clear that to live you need to grow in all that you do.

Now that LIFE has a clearer picture on your mind and you sort of understand it better, we are closer to understanding what 'success' is.

Success, hence, is the ability to execute & grow with consistent consistency (in all that you are a part of) with your given abilities, situations, constraints & requirements.

One quote that would stand out to support this lesson is "One's acceptance of one's own ability should be right and truthful& by no means be compared to anyone else's or anything else". Majority try to claim more abilities than they actually possess and end up strained, stressed and defeated with low morale. So my suggestion to you all—Accept your present potential and as you walk ahead in life—it shall only grow with each little effort of yours towards loving life and meetings it's challenges.

LIFE:

Lousy **I**f **F**ailed **E**xpectations

*L*ovely *I*f *F*inite *E*xpectations

*L*egendary *I*f *F*ulfilled *E*xpectations

*L*ive *I*t *F*or*E*nsuring

It's

*L*abelled *I*nspirational *F*or *E*veryone

If you are born to a poor family, it is your given set up with defined constraints, & when you move forward executing to your best each time, you shall sooner or later stand comparable in your achievements & abilities to all your role models you think have achieved a lot more and were blessed with right resources & circumstances.

Remember *"Start is fate, but the end is your right."*

The speed of growth that you achieve depends on your motivation/inspiration/drive which comes from the desires and the desire to achieve your dreams, which comes from how deeply you connect to your dreams, which is finally a result of multiple intentions/objectives/ values/beliefs which further combines all important governing factors for the growth of happiness in your life.

Eventually it's best to end this chapter on the note *that LIFE is the second name for GROWTH; not growth of money, fame, name or talents alone, but of anything that you are involved in and you aim to achieve.*

Put down Your thoughts/feelings here so far.

(You can be random but be honest in writing things here, not about the book, but those thoughts/feelings about yourself, your dreams, your visions, your life that got triggered so far while reading this.)

With Mr. Michael Teoh in Yaroslavl, Russia.

Michael Teoh has been the Smaller Earth Ambassador for 2011 Your Big Year Competition. He is an entrepreneur from Malaysia who has travelled the world impacting millions of people at 25.

Visit Michaelteoh.com for details

At the London Eye, UK, during the YOUR BIG YEAR Competition (March 2012).

Put down Your thoughts/feelings here so far.

(You can be random but be honest in writing things here, not about the book, but those thoughts/feelings about yourself, your dreams, your visions, your life that got triggered so far while reading this.)

When you practice
leadership,
The evidence of
quality of your
leadership,
Is known from the
type of leaders that
emerge out of
your leadership . . .

3: 2 Faces of LIFE: Success & Failure!

Now that you understand Success, quite rightly failure is opposite of that. But unlike success, failure is best defined in reference to goals and targets we take.

So, what is a target? How do you take one? A target, set to be achieved, is an object of transport to help you reach from where you are to where you eventually plan to be.

Majority of people are pushed down completely by this thing called failure and they never rise again in life. Here I would love to clarify through my personal experience that Life doesn't stop no matter how many times you fail, likewise the spirit of trying/attempting should never stop no matter how many times you fail. With this being the core of our discussion I would love to share the most valuable lesson of my life that

"A failure of execution of one of your targets doesn't guarantee that you fail to reach your aspirations, neither does success of any of your intermediate steps guarantee your final dreams to be achieved."

Life is a chain of events executed in a way which is - most convenient to 'you', 'your' dreams & people 'you' desire to be with & people you have been put up to live with . . .

It's a balance that one needs to achieve that one shouldn't get carried away when he/she achieves smaller targets & neither lose morale on failing a few of them.

Many people ask me this question "Success cannot guarantee further success, then why does failure still hurt?" This is exactly the lesson that I wish to share with you all, that since success cannot guarantee you further success & it can only create scope for further progress & it's your performance each time that keeps you on top, likewise no failure can keep you down and under forever or for too long.

Failure is an essential part of this journey called LIFE. It's closer to Growth than success itself is. Failure is the one that makes lessons unforgettable & registers them in long-term memory unlike success which relies on temporary cache. A foundation with just success is wet& weak, while the one on failure is firm & strong.

Just how, day & night make 24 hours complete, success & failure make this journey of life complete. Always remember a continued journey after a failure (taking ahead the lessons learnt from the failure & implementing the necessary corrections) is a clear

At times what you expect and what happens don't match. The faster you accept and adapt to what happened & work towards creating what you believed, that what you expected gets created in a whole new way . . !

call for success in itself and visits success as one of its definite pit stops.

There is enough proof for us to learn from men of great honour & rank, who made great things happen despite series of failures. Most of us know that after repeated failures Abraham Lincoln became the president, so did Thomas Alva Edison invent bulb, while Apple innovated the ipod design similarly after series of failures and Microsoft developed windows that is opening doors for massive works across the globe happen.

Every success story follows the EAST principle—
Endure, Accept, Survive & Thrive.

So, on a concluding note for this chapter, just embed this deep on your mind:

"Any Failure in life is no end, it's just a bend!"

Put down Your thoughts/feelings here so far.

(You can be random but be honest in writing things here, not about the book, but those thoughts/feelings about yourself, your dreams, your visions, your life that got triggered so far while reading this.)

Life is simple, keep it that way!

When going gets tough, the tough get going!
Once the tough get going the rest follow the Leaders!!!

Put down Your thoughts/feelings here so far.

(You can be random but be honest in writing things here, not about the book, but those thoughts/feelings about yourself, your dreams, your visions, your life that got triggered so far while reading this.)

Relationships is not
a game of amateurs
is what people say . . .

But they begin to
foster between
amateurs &
become a reason to
make them
matured grown-ups!

4: Passion & Determination!

After great lessons on LIFE, Success and failure, time to learn what makes success happen. Of course, none of you would be interested to learn what makes failure happen? If you still wish to then it's pretty easy—close this book! ☺

In this chapter I address the most critical issue this generation faces, the greatest prevailing confusion/ question among the majority lot of us is "To follow your heart or NOT?". If yes, then how do we know what our heart is passionate about, is it our inner calling or not? A staggeringly big question hence stands in front of us "What is passion?"

Then the question which tonnes of them ask me—"How do I discover my passion?" is naturally something that would need attention. But besides all this, an interesting term that tags along with these terms is *Determination*. "You need to be determined to make things happen" | "Determination is the key to success" | "If you are

Leadership is all
about caring, daring
and sharing!

Caring for people,
Daring to Act
fearlessly,
&
Sharing the
success with all!

passionate about something you got to be determined to make it happen" are statements we often hear.

In previous chapters our discussions helped us conclude that "*failure is not the end of the road, it is just the bend in the road*". The one thing that validates this statement & makes you see success as a sure shot destination in your life is determination.

> **"Determination is the ability to stick to your decision with all your heart & execute what you are doing to your possible best &fullest, until you achieve what you desire to."**

You want to become a doctor, a sport-star, a cine-star or anything for that matter, you need to GO FOR IT until you make it happen, no matter what the world has on its tongue about you and your desires. The bottom-line is "*There is no looking back*"—that's determination.

A lot of people feel that it is difficult to achieve such levels of determination, let alone success which cometh later. On the contrary, I feel, it is way too easy to achieve high levels of determination once what you are pursuing is your passion or a part of your passion or leads towards something that is your passion. When you are interested

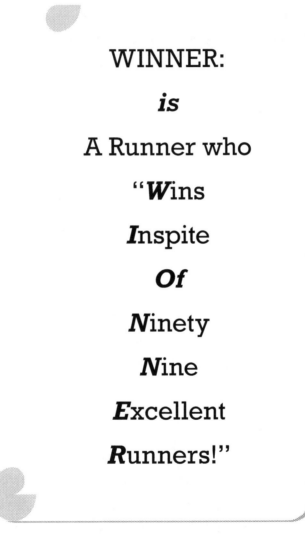

WINNER:

is

A Runner who

"*W*ins

*I*nspite

Of

*N*inety

*N*ine

*E*xcellent

*R*unners!"

in something you are turned on during the pursuit, It is these interests turned into commitment that determine how deeply and strongly you execute something.

What tires us up and what doesn't is just a result how committed or interested we are in something.

Again there is a very thin line between interest and commitment. *Interests change, commitments don't; they are fulfilled.* People change what they are interested in not what they are committed to or convinced about or what they are passionate for. Hence the best way to develop the ability to stick to what you are doing is to ensure you are passionate about it.

This brings us to our questions "What is passion? How do we get passionate about something? How do we learn about our passions?"

Of what I have understood in life, this far, as I stand passionate (deeply interested rather committed) towards a large number of things, executing each one of them really well, I have figured out that there are 2 ways to learn about your passions or develop them:

a. *One is you know you are passionate about something by the deep interest the activity*

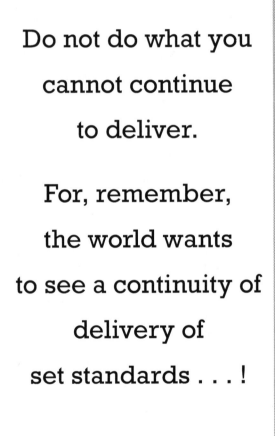

Do not do what you
cannot continue
to deliver.

For, remember,
the world wants
to see a continuity of
delivery of
set standards . . . !

triggers in you each time you are involved in it, by default without much mental efforts of pushing yourself to doing it.

b. *Another is when you are focussed on to a work, developing interesting sides to it and you are continuously growing your depth of interest towards the objectives and goals of the work, you eventually (due to long-term involvement in it) develop a deep interest towards the work which evolves to become one of things you are passionate about.*

There is a very nice quote applicable for the latter and that is **"You love something, do it, you don't love, don't do it, but when you are doing something you better LOVE IT!"**

Now coming to the question of *"how does one know what he/she is passionate about?"* Based on (a)—The best way to find out your passions or rather discover, is to put your hands into a number of things in early stages of your life. It's in your early stages of life, that you know career is still a distant thing and parents are your guardians.

Discovering
While Doing
Is Natural . . .

But,

Doing

Immediately

After Discovering

Is The

Attitude of Winners!

A few of the things you step into will stand out to interest you strongly. When you begin pursuing all of those things that interest you continuously, few of them will die out with time and few will continue driving you deeper and deeper. It's those that drive you deeper with time that you are passionate about &you shouldn't hesitate endorsing them as your career or lifetime fields of work and research.

Based on what we discussed in point (b)—the route I discovered is the greatest lesson of my life, my strongest experience. The story is of one of my full-time career today, it's an area of my life, though a prominent career of mine, I did not know I was even interested in when I started.

Public speaking is what I am talking about and now even writing for that matter. The reason I got really passionate about both of these was owing to one of the things I learnt from my mentors, as mentioned before as well: *"You love something, do it, you don't love something, do not do it, but when you are doing something you better LOVE it!"*.

My mentors always taught me to do things with a lot of enthusiasm & love for it, or rather in one

Travel

Moulds A Man,

People

Mould His Wisdom

And

Experiences

Mould His

LIFE . . . !

word—passionately. Hence, I went on to take passionate speeches wherever I got a chance to as I was involved into a business that needed public presence pretty often. During this journey of delivering speeches, the responses I received killed my doubts and I realised soon enough that I was a good speaker. The responses were overwhelming & they drove me further till I became what I am today. Am still driven!

Later, I got determined to be one of the best public speakers of my times. As I continue my efforts towards the same, I write this to you today, standing as a speaker who has already inspired more than a million people in various parts of the world from all walks of life ranging from age 5 to 75.

From marketing to sales to leadership to memory techniques to relationships to emotional intelligence to business development to tourism I have delivered speeches on about anything including "How to live a happy married life?" to over 50 couples at the age of 23, when I wasn't married. The talk was indeed a grand success. I feel blessed and honoured to know that I am a listed speaker in the esteemed & reputed Moscow Speakers Bureau, when once I know I had walked out of

Let
All Your
Life's
Experiences
Lead
To More
Writing
&
Encourage
More Reading..!

selections for a debate competition in my college days thinking I stood no chance looking at the rest.

So, if you are already doing something and do not know what your passions are, **take a goal of being the best of what you are doing, start discovering the interesting sides of your pursuit,** after all, everything on this earth can be made interesting, Soon you will get deeply interested in what you are doing. Then, just get determined to be the best in your field amongst all those who belong to your trade/profession.

If you are appearing for an exam, be the best to pass out; if you are a teacher, take the target to have the highest no of students who are deeply overwhelmed with your teaching; if you are a businessman, take the target to stand out as a brand in your product arena; if you are a doctor, be the best one morally and by means of your service; if you are a sports star, take the challenge to win the titles in the upcoming Olympics or any other titles and so on. No matter which field you are in, strive to be the best! Better than your yesterday.

Once you are determined to be the best in what you are passionate about, Success would find your address even if you were to be hiding in the darkest corners of this

When every minute of your day is planned & you are packed for days, you shall soon realize that the pain of past fades, vision of life gets clearer and all that seemed to poison your life Ceases to exist.

earth, even if you were lying down in your living room or you were sleeping away to glory after a spell of mind blowing effort towards your goals or you just changed your address☺.

This more or less, in the shortest notes of mine, sums up what I wish to communicate to you about what life is, its purpose, what success is, how failure meets us on the way and eventually how we could discover our passion and be determined about making it big.

But, all that we discussed would be incomplete without converting your journey towards your visions/dreams into goals and targets. We shall take this deeply in the next chapter, but for now I end this chapter re-iterating

"You love something, do it, you don't love something, do not do it, but when you are doing something you better LOVE IT!"

There is no option—

WE HAVE TO WIN!
We are BORN FOR IT!
We have to do it!
WHO ELSE WILL IF NOT US?

Put down Your thoughts/feelings here so far.

(You can be random but be honest in writing things
here, not about the book, but those thoughts/feelings
about yourself, your dreams, your visions, your life
that got triggered so far while reading this.)

Put down Your thoughts/feelings here so far.

(You can be random but be honest in writing things here, not about the book, but those thoughts/feelings about yourself, your dreams, your visions, your life that got triggered so far while reading this.)

"You are the only one who could stop yourself from reaching your goals & fulfilling your desires! Beware!!!"

5: GOALs—most VITAL!

A football match between Liverpool & Manchester United would be breath-taking any day, but would be the most futile one, if there were no goal posts on either side. Teams would go on playing forever to no conclusion aimlessly. Hence, a life without goals is like a football game without goalposts, a race without an end, a journey without a destination, a word without definition& overall it's a LIFE without any direction!

Life can't be directed & progress cannot be measured without goals. A lot of people shoot this question at me (I am still alive☺) *"Why are goals this important? Can't one just go on working endlessly?"* My answer is simple— besides being a measure for progress goals are a reason for motivation and drive to achieve our visions and dreams, they serve the purpose to realign us each time we are diverted like the horse's blinders.

To the one who doesn't know where he wants to reach, every inch covered is a destination achieved.

All have dreams,
live for them,
They add meaning
to LIFE.

The only thing that
differentiates us
from other beings is
the fact that us can
DREAM!!!

Setting goals and targets hence is the most important part of the game called LIFE. Imagine running without a boundary line, imagine an exam without TIME-UP deadline, imagine a text-book with unlimited pages, a subject with unlimited syllabus etc. All these are absurd just like the football game. Hence having a goal is vital, pivotal for career and a great life.

A lot of people ask me, how to develop self confidence? While, Confidence is a result of consistently achieving your targets, Self confidence is nothing but the belief in yourself that you are capable of doing what you are taking up, which comes by results of past which motivate you for future endeavours. When in past you have taken up things and accomplished them successfully it always makes you remind yourself of the adage—"Once a winner, winner for a lifetime" Remember it doesn't matter how small or big the targets achieved were, as long as they were taken and accomplished.

E.g., If you have about 15 units of work to be done (15 chapters to study, 15 projects to complete, 15 sales to be accomplished, 15 presentations to do etc) & you have 30 days left. Then in simple steps just take a target of completing 10 units of work in first half of time i.e.,

A

Controlled

Mind

Can

Create

All

That

It

Words . . . !

in first 15 days, which should be further broken to 6 in first 8 days and 4 in next 7 days. The last 5 units can be finished in next 8 days which leaves 7 days as a buffer time for contingency.

More check points allow for a few rearrangements in the deadlines so that the final deadline is achieved right and well. Work completed well within time, fills you up with self esteem and high levels of confidence for all that is coming ahead! Hence, goals broken down into simpler targets make things happen in much faster pace than estimated.

A few manipulations of deadlines is permissible, as it's human to anticipate failures. But largely this gives you the ability to plan well and decide deadlines. Deadlines are a reason for producing focussed workforce and it's a definite secret of achievers.

Excessive manipulations in the deadlines is always bad, as that induces the attitude of procrastination, which a majority of us have been victims of, somewhere in the past or are even today (did you just smile☺?). The attitudes of giving up/quitting also develop when you foster the habit of manipulating your own deadlines.

A focussed
Mind is a result
Of a little
Effort
To tell Your
Distractions
To sleep for
A couple of hours
While you are at
WORK

Another little weapon during the battle of life is this great attitude of *not taking yourself for granted* and being ready to *punish yourself if you have gone wrong.* Once you take a target, be strict with yourself. It is a great attitude to have.

Punishing yourself on failing the target is a great practice(No suicides please—Just punish, don't kill yourself☺), e.g., sacrificing your favourite Tv serial/ chocolate/ game/ talking to a friend for a week/ fortnight/10 days etc. Is a punishment you must give yourself in order to get more done from yourself.

Given the fact that you punish yourself for failing, you should also learn to reward yourself when you complete a target. *Treating yourself is a great practice,* it boosts your morale.

*"How do we set goals? What is the best way to set goals?"*All said & done, technically your goals of course need to follow the brilliant & best prevailing norm of being SMART

S—Specific
M—Measurable
A—Achievable
R—Realistic
T—Time Bound

Have a **GOAL** to
keep the following
5-'H' OUT of your life
H – Harass
H – Hamper
H – Hurt
H – Harm
H – Hinder
To
Ensure H=Happiness
Prevails forever!

Examples of SMART Goals:

I shall complete 5 chapters in 7 days.

I shall complete 3 subjects for this year in 3 months.

I shall complete my sales target for today in next 4 hours.

I shall buy a blue Audi car worth 0.5 Million in next 2 years.

I shall buy an apartment worth 1 Million $ before turning 30.

Examples of goals that aren't SMART:
I shall complete all subjects in one day.

I shall study 5 chapters in 2 hours.

I shall complete my education as soon as possible.

I shall buy a large house (or a big car).

Once you ensure your goals are SMART, the most important thing to remember is that the drive and motivation to make your dreams happen and achieve your goals comes from your VISION/WHY—your purpose of life. No matter what, you need to pump yourself towards your GOAL. Any added inspiration or motivation acts like Nitrous oxide cylinders to boost your speed of execution. So keep yourself motivated & inspired all the time. Stay on toes to make things happen.

Remember if you have not defined your deadlines, haven't decided how much you would want to accomplish in how much time, you definitely are moving into blank space and achieving any amount of growth in life is impossible.

If you are still confused on any of this, Do not worry, it's not abnormal—A few more repeated readings of what you have read from page 1 till here, will definitely help you gain clarity. It's like when a movie is watched thrice, it has all its misunderstood or skipped scenes understood and grabbed. Likewise re-reading this book will be of utmost help to get deeper clarity. Besides, you could also consult a good life coach for more help in this regard.

Your goals are yours and none can alter your decision to reach it. Though there are enough people in the market to make your visions get blurred as you walk along the path of making your dreams happen, if you stick long enough, they are bound to materialize into realities of your life. Stay clear and stay focussed.

They say:
"A vision with clarity is a vision to reality!"

What has this chapter added to all that you have felt, thought and written before? It's time to record it before you forget and get lost in your thoughts & lose track of where you started from and why. I do not want you to make this as another book which is now your target to complete.

If you are truly reading this book and following the instructions and jotting things down in these pages, you can never finish this book, IT ALL STARTS HERE! Lets simplify LIFE! Go ahead, Write your mind here!

It indeed is always overwhelming to see the responses of the crowds after my talks! What matters more is the impact they take away! I always tell them,

Life changes the way we decide it to!

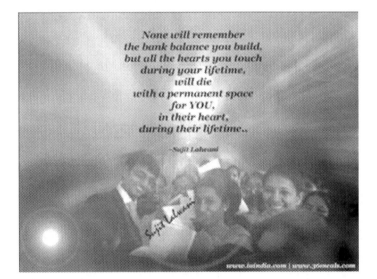

Being honoured after I delivered a talk on
"how to live a happy married life!".
I wasn't married then; what I did realize was that it takes
an observer to understand people & relations, but it
takes love and egoless behaviour to maintain them.
I guess I luckily had both of them then! Thanks to
my parents and the culture they nurtured in me.
In the picture is my Dad collecting the
token of honour with pride

Make a list of all the problems that you think are hindering your growth & progress in life.

(Small or Big—Just make note, Only then read ahead).

6: Problems . . .

LIFE—Success—Failure—Passion—Determination—Goals and now let us finally talk about the greatest attention seeking child of LIFE☺—PROBLEMS!

After everything is understood, An important thing that still remains a mystery is PROBLEMS. How do we face them? How do we keep ourselves positive forever & be happy? (this question in itself is a problem—A BIG ONE! ☺)

Folks, problems are just those elements of life, which come to tell us or teach us something *we do not know*. It's just one of the ways LIFE lets you know, that you need to GROW. In fact, they are signboards for growth in our life. The purpose of life as discussed is growth and problems indeed are a definite indication that you are growing.

If you aren't facing problems you can be sure you have down-sized your dreams, you have accepted to be a mediocre in what you are doing, you have killed your

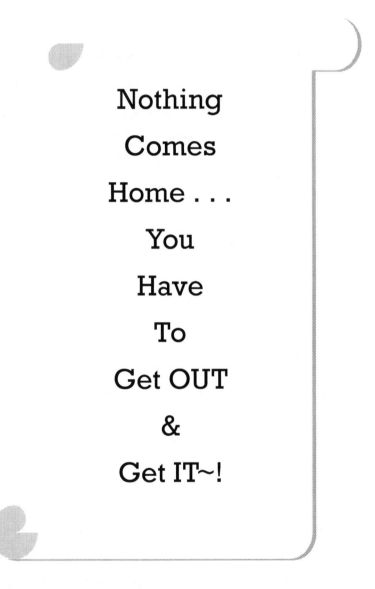

Nothing

Comes

Home . . .

You

Have

To

Get OUT

&

Get IT~!

dreams that make you feel your life is worth living; you are not breathing, you aren't making or aren't able to put efforts to grow at all.

Even a single dream that you are willing to work for
is sufficient to let you know that
problems are a permanent part of life.

ALL problems can never be solved, for, they are the only locomotives to take our life ahead and drive us towards our dreams and desires. But, by most of us & most of the times they are perceived as road blocks instead of *growth catalysts*. Instead of rejoicing at every signboard of growth, we are busy complaining about them. I don't understand why? Simple—we want easier ways out or we have a certain picture of life in our mind with which the situations/circumstances don't match or let's accept it in the face and agree to it—We are lazy!(if you are complaining all the time then it's laziness!)

The reason people perceive problems as road blocks is because they do not address them & keep facing them repeatedly, for, they keep coming till you get over them.

When you face the same problem over and over again, then it's being a road block instead of being a growth

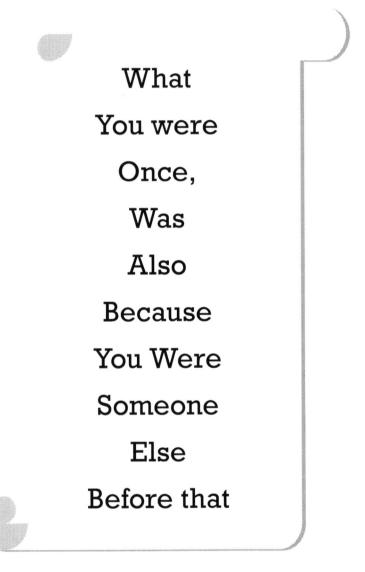

What
You were
Once,
Was
Also
Because
You Were
Someone
Else
Before that

catalyst. If you quickly address an issue and jump to the next, then the problems begin to act as wheels of your wagon, they act as the accelerator pedal of your car, they act as the propeller of your rocket, they act as the CPU of your computer, they act as the battery of your machine, and they rapidly augment the rate of your growth in your pursuit.

Hence in simple words:

"A problem is that element of life, which tells you what you do not have in you to achieve what you want in life."

Problem showcases to you an inability that needs to be addressed. A sharpened axe cuts trees, but when it loses its sharpness, "sharpening it" is the solution to the problem but it is the solution only when the desire to cut more trees exists. Sharpening the axe is futile if the desire to cut more trees itself doesn't exist.

Now that you understand what a problem is and the fact that it is great to have them, beware of the problems that are like viruses in the system. They eat up the CPU itself. One among those that is commonly faced is the PEER PRESSURE.

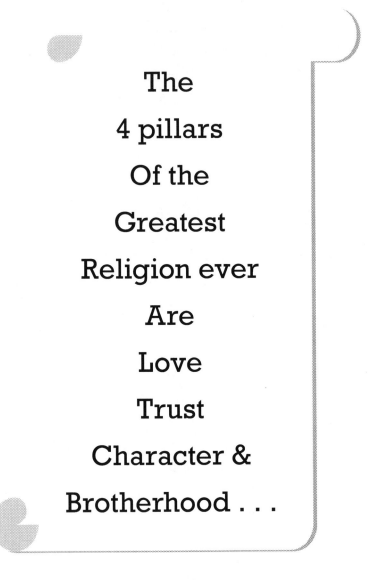

The

4 pillars

Of the

Greatest

Religion ever

Are

Love

Trust

Character &

Brotherhood . . .

But if you see it from all angles and analyze it carefully, even peer pressure is just a problem to be addressed. From our mentioned definition of problem, we know a problem is just an inability to handle something; hence, handling people is also a problem only until you have an inability to handle them. A lot of people are bogged down by worries of what others think about them. Friends, I urge you all to ignore this continuing and perennial thought of "what others think about you" and focus on developing your strengths, dreams, abilities and talents. Peer pressure can't govern your decisions if your beliefs are strong, but owing to low self morale you tend to get driven into the whirlpool of opinions of people around you and hence this pressure takes over in different ways.

If taunts and comments of people are a problem, it's just the little sportive nature you need to develop in yourself, where you need to tell yourself, it's just a part and parcel of life, which you have to inevitably go through to GROW. When you know your dreams, with utmost clarity, and are determined to achieve them, you may not even have the time to focus on what people think about or comment about you.

Once
You keep
Aside the
Emotional side
Of yours,
Is whe
ou sto
sing the phrase
"This was a BAD
PHASE" of life..

E.g., At this moment I truly do not care, what a million others are thinking about me while I write this book to you. All of them put together couldn't stop me from compiling this book for you & it has reached you through all barriers. People kept talking, while I kept writing. Remember *"What you focus on, expands!"* So don't over-focus on your problems else they will blow out of proportion. Focus on solving them.

"Peers put pressure on those peers who are available to be put pressure upon. If you are busy chasing your dreams you may never face the brunt of this, but if you are lazy and spending away your time on things of no value and return, you are worth being made fun of"

You are worth being made fun of if you simply wiling away your time, because you would find yourself doing the same to others in your free-time.

> *"Do not do to others what you would not want others to do unto you!".*

I advise you to drown in the beauty of dreams of this beautiful life and endlessly walk towards them. Dreams have the power to move you from being ordinary to extra-ordinary; chase them and you shall discover that

The

Glory

Is

Always

Hidden

Between

The

Lines

Of the

Story

your sense organ EAR was never engineered to receive taunts and comments.

When it comes to talking about problems, I would love to quote here about an article of mine, I once wrote for the e-Magazine of IU(iuemag.com) with the title "LIFE— An ever changing question paper!", whose theme was— *Each time you think you have got all the answers to all your worries/problems/questions in life, Life changes the question paper itself.*

This made me understand that I need to be ever ready for challenges. A new set of challenges shall appear each time I finish a given set of them. While dealing with peer pressures, problems & challenges I concluded the greatest empowering truth of my life:

"The most important learning of my life is that no matter what stage of life you are at, what position you are in, what profession you are in, people will never be satisfied with you—someone somewhere will surely be dissatisfied with you, and only then you can be sure you are on the right track."

It's impossible to satisfy everyone's expectations in your life. So I decided to just cater to those of the closest

Reputation

I

Temporary . . .

As

Much as

The

Ma

wning

You

eputation Is

and most loved ones, which also has its own challenges which are unique to each of our lives.

A lot of times the expectations of close ones kill us more than taunts and comments of our enemies. It's true &I totally agree. It's definitely the case, when you are failing them continuously, but under such cases you need to know where to draw the line. Expectations of people from you itself is a chapter that we could deal separately, but in a nutshell it could be understood by going back to our chapter on failures and success.

I would love to remind you here, that whatever you are doing and expected to do (expectations of close & loved ones), if you make it your passion and do it with love and then be determined to be the best, you will soon see people giving you more freedom to do all that you desire than you ever imagined!

Expectations are pressures world puts on you, because they think you are capable of keeping upto them. It's a positive thing(under limits of course) which should empower you to understand that you are worthy of being expected from.

Restating here and closing this chapter:

"Problems are a mere indicator that
you are growing& moving ahead.
They need to be addressed &not complained about!"

Now you finally have a changed perception towards your problems in life. Time to note down this change that has taken place. Go back to your list of problems and write down the way your perception towards them has changed!

(Note: Re-read the chapter if any particular problem is still bothering you and feel the change take place. If you still are bothered, feel free to contact me at sujitlalwani.com)

You are by now a BELIEVER!

Write your dreams here that you commit yourself to!

If you ask me why I love my life,

its because I find awesome satisfaction in serving . . .

. . . I had everything, they had nothing . . . .

. . . They had a smile; the only thing I didn't have . . .

But, after serving them I feel complete . . .

**Make time to serve mankind and do things that
cannot be repaid in cash/kind . . .**

Every comforting
word is a command
from a man of
action . . .

While every word of
command is
commotion from a
man of just words . . .

By the way I am a Man of Action!

7: Patience is the Virtue!

It definitely is easy said than done, that patience is the virtue. It definitely is easy, for those who can be patient. For the rest patience is in itself a goal to be accomplished on the to-do list. (Did I notice another smile on your face? Am sure you are able to recall all those times, when you put down your resolutions and one of them was— Need to be more patient, have better temperament, or better control on emotion & we lost patience before we could achieve it each time ☺)

Why is it that some people are able to be extremely patient while the rest of them get restless pretty soon? As I promise to simplify life here, I would bring you very close to understanding what patience is in the simplest way possible.

Just as salt & sugar are universal ingredients, that truly bring taste, but they needn't be yet added in every single dish. Likewise patience & determination are two such qualities that bring taste to life, though they may at times not be needed in all situations. It's time now

Patience Pays . . .
Is true!

But the greater
Truth is tha
It take
Advance payment
Before it paying
In return!

that you look into the definition of patience that would encompass a majority of its wings for our simplified life:

"Patience is the ability to stay optimistic about the change you desire, ability to wait for the result you wish to see, keeping hope for the desired to happen & continue working towards the goal, having situations & people respond opposite but still not forget that reacting or over-reacting with loss of patience would cost more than payoff. Its overall the ability to face the adversities of any form in the face and throw them a smile that conveys to them, that you don't care about them & they are unable to cause pain they desire to till adversities actually get convinced.

You fake it all to your possible best till you can take it all. When you have faked it a lot of times, it becomes a natural attitude and being perseverant till doing it all becomes natural is what is best understood of 'patience'!"

After this lovely piece of detailed definition of patience, if you still have questions on your mind to what exactly is patience—then just need to fake it, face it & take it ☺ ! Did you just lose patience? If not, then you have developed it ☺☺

Without the desire
to be patient
patience doesn't
happen,
Just like without
the desire to grow,
LIFE doesn't happen!

Jokes apart, let's take it right—it's important to know that it's not failure to be unable to keep patience at times, as long as you are conscious about developing it, you are on the right track. Stay focussed by reminding yourself of what you wish to be and what you wish to do.

Each time you lose it and remind yourself and regain strength to keep track of life and get focussed with your energies being spent in the direction of your goals, you are actually getting more patient.

It's definitely not wrong that someone claimed "patience pays!" It's pretty simple for me to answer if you ask me why. The answer is this story which I am reminded of, where a stone crusher would be giving his shots on the stone to crush a large stone that was deemed the toughest rock. On a fine morning after months of trying to break the stone, after about a 100 hits that morning the stone breaks apart and he is called the strongest man around the town.

For years, they relied on him for breaking such tough rocks/stones, and they kept analysing his food habits and health habits to discover his secrets of strength. Before late they realized that he was as normal as

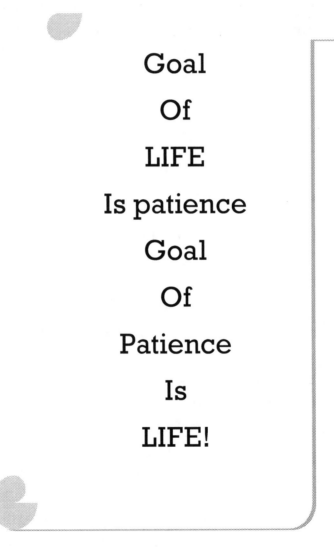

Goal

Of

LIFE

Is patience

Goal

Of

Patience

Is

LIFE!

anyone else, while his strength lay in his ability to keep hitting the stone, till it broke apart. It's the adversity that lost patience against him.

The strength is in your ability to keep hitting against the stones in your life that are deemed the toughest. Remember they are all man-made, if someone can, you too can.

They aren't tougher than your will-power. Keep HITTING! Not on the next door girl though, else you shall be hit in return ☺ Jokes apart, hope you are patiently able to go through this piece of text. Just keep pushing yourself page after page and you shall soon come to the close of this book before you realize it's done and I am pretty sure half of it if applied could mean a simplified life.

Patience:

Powerful **A**bility

To **I**nduce

Energy

N

Continuing **E**nthusiasm

Now, you have added patience to your dreams! All that seemed like a herculean task will now seem achievable. You are STRONG & firm.
Time to put down your plan of action here!

You are STRONG & firm.

Time to put down your plan of action here!

You are STRONG & firm.

Time to put down your plan of action here!

8: Do I Follow my heart or continue my present career path?

The name of this book is Life Simplified and hence I do not want to take pages together to answer this one, though you would love it for the price you have paid. But then the additional price that you would end up paying is for the amount of time you would lose reading redundant stuff added to increase the mass of this book, which is clearly not my goal. I expect to see your life simplified as I close this chapter with a few powerful paragraphs.

When I look back at my life today, I am glad that the best talents have once worked with me when I was working in networking marketing industry. Me & my supremely talented brother together lead the network of diverse talents and am glad the journey continues even after jumping over from the network marketing arena into the real time entrepreneurship arena. It's a pleasure to see people who say that they are in a fix doing things they don't love and we help them discover their passion in no

Follow Your

Heart

&

The world

Shall

Follow YOU!

Reject it and

It stops beating!

time. It's all about getting out there and doing it, than thinking or talking about it. It's all about EXPLORING!

I am glad that today the best talents are working with me with patience and hope of a great future, which they are able to derive looking at my life closely & they know their lives are far too simplified working towards what they are passionate about than working somewhere where their soul wouldn't just establish a connection.

The best part about discovering your passion is like the mobile network system. Each time your soul is found working in a place where your inner calling isn't there, your soul shouts *connection error* or *network doesn't exist* or *it's out of coverage area*. Hence, next time you try connecting to your soul and it isn't in the coverage area or answers switched off, you can be sure, it's not your inner calling. You might be getting paid more but life is heading towards being just more meaningless and lifeless.

It's true that responsibilities, at times, that bind you and the uncertainties that following your heart brings along stop you from making your decisions. But friend, to make life meaningful doesn't mean leaving your present job/career path or quitting it and then following your

Life Is 'Simple' By Nature . . .

The deeper you try to study, the more you complicate it. Just believe in its simplicity & it shall show you it is far too Simple actually!

heart, it simply means keep your heart functional while your other organs are doing their job respectively.

When once the timing is right let all other organs follow the heart! But till then let the heart beat at least! **Don't kill hope! KEEP PATIENCE! Fake it if needed**, you will soon develop it & find yourself following your heart. A strong stone would be crushed with your faith and you would be regarded in the list of strongest men in town.

Trust me friend, today when I am being looked upto as a star, I just sometimes can't comprehend what is it that I did that made me one and the answer is *"walked long enough when all others by then had stopped for tea-breaks and some even changed their track itself!"*

It's simply about exploring, learning, experiencing your passions in all the free time you get or rather time you are willing to make to develop the necessary expertise to be sure to jump into the world of your passion that you are able to assure yourself that you could sustain yourself and your family with what you earn.

As long as you are able to design an earning model for your sustenance and that of your family to begin with, it's a great model to begin following your heart. Growth

Time is too short in this one life, to be able to do everything, but it definitely is long enough at least to be able to develop the will to do anything & everything . . .

follows. For questions on how to grow, patiently go back to the chapter now on growth and life, and reiterate those words on your mind and you shall see the depth to which you would be able to catch what is written there. It would all begin to make deep sense now!

The best book I have ever read that I would love to quote here is *"Follow your heart"* by Andrew Matthews. If you could grab one of this, please ensure you do. It's possibly the most powerful content and deeply influential in itself. No other text could ever give me the amount of clarity this book brought into me.

Finally, on a concluding note, I would love to share that just **decide where you are heading, what your vision for life is, decide how you would want to leave this world, decide what you would want to be remembered for when you leave this planet, decide what your tomb-stone would read when you are no more.** I decided and it powerfully moves me every single day and I hope before I close this text you too do the same . . .

I want to die with my tomb-stone shouting
(if I am burnt to ashes, my ashes shall do the shouting)
"The world once knew a man,
Who made a difference to the man-kind every
single day of his life, till he lived his last breath!"

Finally here I come to the end of this short book. I am truly hoping that the content here was simple and easy to imbibe and execute. I would love to end with these lines:

I know the time is too short in this life, to be able to do everything, but it definitely is long enough to develop at least the 'will' to be able to do anything & everything.

Once that WILL develops, A new story worth reading happens, generations are left with a story they could learn from, foot-prints are created on the sands of time that are worth following, trails are left on the oceans of the life that guide the upcoming sailors, paths are tread through the thick forests of life making way for others to follow &eventually the vastness is resolved by the threads of simplicity—
In 4 words LIFE IS THEN SIMPLIFIED!

If your life or perceptions of life are simplified after reading this book I would love to hear your story at sujitlalwani.com

You are ALL SET!

The clear measure of your growth would be, when you learn something new, from each chapter, on each of your re-visit to the book. If you do not learn something new each time, it simply means you haven't done much in that period of time, that could amount to adding to your experience & hence, re-reading of the book seem to have given the same lesson again.

So Just decide your next date of reading this book again & get into action to measure your growth!

For now, Promise yourself to keep revisiting the quotes on the left every single day while you are working your heart out!

Date:

It was lovely talking to you!
Wishing you a **Simply Simplified Life** ahead!

Awaiting your reviews on sujitlalwani.com
(Before you log on to the internet to share your words with me,
I am sure you wish to share your words with me
—Share it here!)

9: Thumb-rules for LIFE!

I conclude this short book with the following thumb-rules:

(Print these out and put it up where you could read them every single day!)

- DREAM BIG | GROWTH is LIFE.
- Make growth your purpose of life.
- Accept failures gracefully.
- Do not get carried away by success.
- Believe in yourself.
- Action leads to result which leads to confidence.
- Make your goals SMART & achieve them.
- Be passionate about all that you do.
- Discover your passions.
- Be determined to be the best in all that you do.
- Problems are indicators of growth.
- Attempt till you succeed. Be Patient!
- Someone somewhere will surely be dissatisfied with you, only then you are on the right track
- Don't get stuck at problems.
- You have one life, make it simple, do not complicate.
- Live to love, not to fight and rebel. In the end:

"Love All, Live Tall"

Write down the first five names that come to your mind & the chapters you think will help them!

You can be a reason to simplify someone else's life!
Go ahead & Share it with them!